Family Matters!

A MEMOIR

STEVE KATES

authorHOUSE®

AuthorHouse™
1663 Liberty Drive
Bloomington, IN 47403
www.authorhouse.com
Phone: 1 (800) 839-8640

Published by AuthorHouse 06/14/2017

ISBN: 978-1-5246-9688-7 (sc)
ISBN: 978-1-5246-9687-0 (e)

Print information available on the last page.

This book is printed on acid-free paper.

"The past is what you remember, imagine you remember, convince yourself you remember or pretend to remember."

Harold Pinter

Tolstoy was wrong - there
ARE no happy families!

Foreword

OKAY, I'LL AMEND MY PREVIOUS statement. There are undoubtedly happy families, but none, I think, without their periods of fears, resentments, disappointments, tragedies, despair, and even unhappiness.

Pure happiness is a Walt Disney, M-G-M myth, which is why their beatific output has been so universally embraced for decades. It's what everyone wants but will never attain. Ozzie and Harriet were a lie!

I have selected incidents from my life which reflect both the laughs and the sad underbellies of my familial connections and interactions. There are good people and good people doing bad things, knowingly or not. There are mean-spirited people. There are pathetic people. There are smart and unintelligent people, both making good and poor choices. And there are failures.

Yet I would wager that if you could have polled the characters herein, 95% of them would say they had happy lives. Perhaps that reflects our miraculous human faculties for self-delusion, survival and, finally, eternal hope.

Some memoirs do not directly mention their author, yet the very narrative can often tell much about the writer - I'm sure many of mine do.

Most of the people in this memoir are gone, and thus defenseless in the face of what my memory has directed me to put on paper. Obviously, my recollections reflect a certain personal bias. But whatever transpired during their lives with me, I wish almost all of them peace.

Contents

325 West End Avenue

IN A 1922 PRIVATELY PRINTED book, "Old New York," there is an aerial photograph of Riverside Drive, which begins at 72nd street heading north in Manhattan along the Hudson River.

In this picture, between 73rd and 74th street sits the Charles Schwab mansion, a vast French Renaissance chateau, occupying an entire city block, surrounded by cast iron fencing, with lawns and gardens wending down towards the drive. Schwab was a founder of Bethlehem Steel and U.S. Steel.

In the background, one block north of that, stands a stately apartment house - 325 West End Avenue - where I spent the majority of my young years, from 4 to 21.

It was one of the oldest buildings on West End Avenue - I still remember the coal chute into the basement to fuel the furnaces. In that same era, my friends and I would "sled" joyfully down the giant mountain of coal outside the Museum of Natural History on 81st street, arriving home looking like rejects from a minstrel show!

There were two separate "wings" of the building. The wing nearer the Hudson had one 11 and one 5 room apartment on each floor. The wing where we lived, facing the Avenue, had 9 and 7 room apartments - we camped out in a mere 7.

The building had its drawbacks. Until the early 50's electrical current was DC, incompatible with many appliances and devices then popular. At one point, we had a converter so we could accommodate electric refrigerators, "record players" and a washing machine. Finally, the building converted to AC, just in time to welcome our first television set.

325 was built for a different era. Our apartment had two master bedrooms and two servants rooms off the kitchen, in which there was a call board which indicated which "chamber" was buzzing for assistance (call buttons in the two bedrooms and the living room, with a floor buzzer under the dining room table).

Constructed in an age when help was cheap and plentiful, the roof of the building also had one bathroom and three extra rooms for additional servants who might not readily be accommodated in an apartment - chauffeurs, for example. The roof also sported an enormous communal laundry, windowed on three sides for light, in the middle housing a huge gas dryer through which laundered bed sheets could be hung and then run through to dry before being ironed. Monday was laundry day and the room was filled with Irish and Polish washerwomen plying their tasks.

My mother purchased a washing machine for the apartment, positing that her maid would spend too much time in the roof laundry gabbing with the other women.

In the vast, low-ceilinged basement was a warren of rooms where trunks, furniture, bikes, files could be stored, each apartment having its own locked cage.

But it wasn't the high ceilings, the enormous rooms, the piped in Muzak to play during dinners or the antiquated but wonderfully functional kitchens that made 325 special; it was the tenants.

On the 6th floor in 9 rooms lived Gene Callahan, a prominent Hollywood Art Director and Production Designer. He had won three Oscars for his Art Direction (for "America, America," "The Hustler," and "The Cardinal"). He was also nominated for an additional Oscar for "The Last Tycoon."

Callahan and his "partner" (this was well before the era of open gay liaisons) were garrulous and delightful company, frequently inviting tenants into their beautifully appointed home, beginning with the 30-foot foyer. There was one large bedroom devoted to the miniatures of the sets that Callahan had designed, mesmerizing to a star-struck young boy.

Directly above us lived the Gottfrieds, a refugee family from Germany who, apparently and quite obviously, were able to transport enormous wealth with them when they arrived on our shores. I can still hear Mrs. Gottfried's stiletto heels clicking on the parquet floors which they did not have covered with either rugs or carpeting. Mrs. Gottfried, in my memory, was still swathed in yards of mink even when we left in June for the summer (apart from a few tenants, the building emptied out for 3 months every summer).

And then we had Mrs. November, from the 10th floor. I never knew her first name. She had been a minor silent screen star, and she looked every inch the role. Tall, hair in a turban, and sunglasses (she had some terrible eye condition) she even made "an entrance" into the elevator, always accompanied by her Irish companion, Annie.. She was an approximation of

Carol Burnett's classic parody of Gloria Swanson in "Sunset Boulevard." Her husband was a stodgy, nattily dressed, polite old man.

Mrs. November, it was reputed, had been a mistress of Nicholas Schenck (who hadn't?) when he was the head of Loew's, the parent company of M-G-M. Occasionally, while sitting in the lobby waiting for a car or cab, Mrs. November would share past moments on the set with Garbo and Pola Negri and, yes, Valentino! More magic.

And then there were the Schwartzes, crowded into the 11-room apartment on the 11th floor, with two additional maids' rooms on the roof for their staff.

Mr. Schwartz made women's hosiery, a lot of women's hosiery, and he did know how to spend. They had two maids and a cook and TWO chauffeurs, one to drive, the other to sit beside him and then hop out to open the door for his passengers. Schwartz also had an estate in Ossining where they kept their horses.

There were three Schwartz offspring, Kay, the eldest, a homely, nerdish girl and the twins, Susan and Tommy. The household was rounded out with two boxers and a Doberman pinscher.

At ten, I had a childhood crush on Susan and invited her to the circus. She accepted and I was thrilled. I took the subway to Madison Square Garden and bought the tickets. But then Mrs. Schwartz called my mother to say Susan couldn't make it - she (Mrs. Schwartz) was not happy about having Susan in such a crowded venue without some sort of adult supervision.

This was my first heartbreak, although it didn't last very long, but it was difficult seeing Susan and her mother in the lobby on so many occasions. I think awkward is the word I want, here.

In the late 50s and early 60s, the Puerto Rican invasion of Manhattan was in full flower. The private town houses down the side streets and directly on the avenue were converted to rooming houses. Many Jewish families on the West Side wee moving east to Park and Fifth Avenues. My parents were among the last to leave, in 1963.

Within a few years, 325 went co-op and the occupants, I'm sure, got some wonderful purchase deals. I've driven by the building from time to time. It still had its marquee, and its magnificent marble lobby. The hedges around the front of the building were gone, but the outside had been pressure cleaned and the auburn brick looked new.

In the late 40's the Schwab mansion was demolished and the Schwab House apartment complex replaced it. A building on 72nd street and West End Avenue had finally been converted back to apartments. During World War II, before the building's completion, it had been commandeered as a veterans hospital.

The street is still beautiful, one of only two in all of Manhattan without a bus line (the other is Park Avenue). Some good things never change.

In The Kitchen Of My Youth

I N THE KITCHEN OF THAT apartment, function was everything, aesthetics totally ignored in a space, designed exclusively for cooks and maids, with no thought that the female tenant, mother, wife, sister, whomever, would actually enter the kitchen other than to interview servants.

It was a complex of one large main room, plus a spacious three-sided pantry and a back hall leading to the service entrance and the two small maids' rooms. Ceiling fixtures, each with one bare bulb, provided raw light, serviceable but hideous, harsh. Reflecting the age of our lovely building, there was a house phone to the lobby so that one could be made aware that one's driver was waiting, or that one's guests had arrived.

The main section had one large window facing north, with an oblique view of the Hudson River. The double panes encased thin chicken wire, installed to prevent the savage westerly winter river winds from shattering glass onto the floor and even into our food. A bland white roll-up shade covered the window.

One entire wall was covered with glass-paned wood cabinets, in which neat stacks of plates, dessert services and various glassware were stored. Incredibly, I can picture those several sets of formal china, but I have totally forgotten what our everyday dishes looked like

The cabinets rose to the full height of the ten foot ceiling. The counters below were of thick butcher block, startling horizontal streaks of caramel color in an otherwise totally white world. Below them were storage cupboards and drawers.

The other walls were covered two thirds of the way up with shiny white porcelain subway tiles, while the remainder of the surface was highly glazed white paint.

The single deep, shelved closet was for storage of provisions, along with brooms, mops, brushes and rubber knee pads for floor scrubbing, washboards, an ironing board and the vacuum cleaner. A table with two chrome chairs sat against the closet wall, used for my early morning breakfasts, food preparation, my mother's brief lunches, when home, and interviewing prospective domestics. Another table directly in front of the large window was used as prep space.

The smaller table faced the double porcelain sink on legs, improbably small for the pots and platters it was supposed to accommodate for washing. The remaining wall was dominated by an ancient gas range, a behemoth of black iron and white porcelain, with six burners, three ovens, a broiler, a drawer for warming dinner plates and another for warming rolls, a marvel of late Victorian design and actually extremely dependable for cooking and baking.

Between the kitchen and the dining room was the pantry, also lined with cupboards holding more sets of dishes and crystal, along with the supply of liquors and wines. It, too, had wooden counters, and an extra double sink. All flooring consisted of tiny white and black hexagonal tiles, like the floors in public toilets and bathhouses.

The kitchens in my friends' apartments had sleek and colorful linoleum floors and modern light fixtures and appliances, while ours was merely a kitchen of a bygone vintage, a serviceable venue for household help. And in my eyes, it was the quintessence of antique ugliness. But that kitchen also served as an appropriate forum for some ugliness expressed over time within its sterile, monochromatic walls.

Helen, a maid employed for seven years during my childhood, would iron laundry on Tuesdays, listening to the radio soap operas, while carefully pressing the bed linens, along with our assorted blouses, undergarments and handkerchiefs. While I had an afternoon snack at the table, she would sling insults at me, and threaten that my father would arrive home and punish me for some infraction she would report to him. "I going tell him you don't do homework today," she threatened. This was one of the pleasures that gave meaning to her boring existence, and my father was all too eager to believe her.

She was Czechoslovakian, with small narrow-set eyes and tree-trunk legs well suited for the heavy cleaning work she was required to do.

My mother had also trained Helen to do some rudimentary everyday cooking and to serve gracefully at table, and my father saw in her a delightful foreign waif, deserving of his erudite tutelage in American culture. He sympathized with her stated longing for her Johnnie, who was away in the service (this was during World War II). It was while serving meals that Helen played on my father's gullibility, always with a cheerful word while passing one course or another, while I sulked at my place, isolated, the only one aware of her true sadistic personality.

It was only several years later that my parents discovered Helen's canny but wholesale thievery of linens, jewelry and even my first watch for which "loss" I had been severely punished. She was creating a trousseau for when her Johnnie came home from the war. I was elated when my father told me Helen had been dismissed.

The kitchen was also a suitably theatrical backdrop when once my father, in a rage of temper at something my mother had said, flung a glass of tomato juice against the white tile wall, shattering the glass and inadvertently creating a grisly scene of slaughter as the tomato juice spread and slid down the walls like spattered blood from multiple knife wounds. I stood frozen, not knowing whether to crouch down or run from the room.

The kitchen was also the unfortunate redoubt for my uncontrollable appetite, where I could forage uncontrolled late at night in the ancient refrigerator for leftovers, adding to my weight thus fueling my already adolescent sense of inadequacy.

It was not all darkness and gloom. That dreary, outdated kitchen was also a warm and loving spot in which I shared and bonded with my mother and grandmother, both excellent cooks.

I can still taste the raw almond cookie batter which I was allowed to lick from the mixer blades, a savory treat; thick, smooth and miraculously sweet and aromatic. I still taste the small individual apple pies my mother made for me, so that I could have more of the crisp, sugary crust than one got in a mere ordinary serving. That sweet cinnamon scent still fills my nostrils on command.

Ah, and my grandmother's bundt coffee cake, yeasty, filled with nuts and raisins. She would let me pound the dough with my fists so that the yeast would make it rise in repeated stages. I looked in wonder at how the dough doubled and trebled in size. And how sweet that cake was when toasted, one or two days later, for breakfast with a glass of cold milk.

My grandmother also made her own chopped liver from scratch. I remember the large wooden bowl into which the sautéed livers, hard-boiled eggs and onions were placed, and her stabbing them with a curved two-bladed chopper that ultimately mashed the ingredients into the tasty pate that was one of her signature specialties. I sat in a chair watching her strong, rhythmic motion as she pulverized the contents of that sturdy bowl.

Those were the glorious days of juicy brisket and pates, rare prime rib roasts, cheese soufflés, thick Irish bacon, and heavy cream from the tops of the delivered milk bottles for coffee and cereals, all of us ignorant of what cholesterol even was, probably including our physicians.

My father enjoyed two or three eggs daily for some sixty-years, along with hefty desserts of exotic French cheeses that oozed along the platters into the accompanying crackers or bread, and he never suffered heart problems until his death at 83 from a massive stroke.

I also look back on my excitement when a dinner party was being prepared. It was then that the hand-embroidered damask cloths and napkins were laid out, the finest china and silver were deployed to the dining table, fresh candles placed in the candlesticks, and crystal water and wine goblets were thoroughly washed and carefully placed at the individual settings, along with lush floral arrangements delivered the same morning. There were also urns of cigarettes, ashtrays, and Ronson lighters on the table.

Our caterer, Georgine, arrived with her crew of servers and a sous chef, and that drab kitchen came alive with the scents of exotic foods and the sounds of crack military precision as Georgine marshaled her forces and got everything ready in perfect time, occasionally sneaking me a morsel of some fragrant dish that would be served to the adult guests.

Our kitchen was a life – sometimes unhappy, sometimes happy, almost always busy, with a character all its own and a history that developed as years went by.

No matter how many physical or psychological removes I made from that spacious and otherwise enjoyable apartment, the complex memories of our kitchen have stayed with me, like the indelible scent of a seductive, but poisonous, perfume on a long-stored piece of clothing.

Unanswered Questions

MY MOTHER AND FATHER RETAINED family secrets in different ways. I say "retained" rather than "kept" because my father could no more keep a secret than a tomcat could remain celibate. But his family memories and experiences were parsed out sparingly, held in, I suspect, more from acute pain than from a desire for secrecy and privacy. And as for my mother and her two sisters, they might as well have worked for the CIA.

I knew that my father's mother, Hinda, was schizophrenic, institutionalized on and off for most of her adult life. I have no knowledge of her other than a hideous studio photograph showing an angular, ugly hag staring at the viewer with a terrifying hatred, like something from an old silent movie. When I was eleven, I tore up that dreadful photograph and threw away the pieces in a garbage receptacle on the street. No one ever mentioned missing it. I never did learn anything about her earlier life.

On one occasion, in a talkative mood, my father shared with me, sorrowfully, perhaps guiltily, the story of how he had taken an apartment for his mother and gone to Macy's to furnish it for her. But within weeks, the apartment was in shambles and it was clear she could not live alone, nor care for herself; I assume her next stop was a direct trip to a facility where, in all likelihood, she died. He was ashamed of her, he resented her disease, and, I think, desperately missed the loving ministrations of a normal, caring mother.

When my grandmother lived with us, my father gave her his seat at the head of the table.

As an interesting and related bit, my father was inordinately interested in the canon of literature related to mental health and mental disease.

My father was intermittently raised by two aunts, sisters who lived next door to one another in Brooklyn - Rose Schwartz and Sadie Stein. I don't even know whose side they were on, although I did know them quite well as I grew up. He loved those aunts as he might a mother. Sadie was married to Max Stein who, with his brother founded the Bali Brassiere Company. Max was an ultra-religious tyrant who, while donating millions to Jewish charities, reveled in the rewards gleaned from owning second-mortgages on Harlem tenements. Being a Cohen (a Hebrew priestly caste), he could not stay inside for my father's funeral.

Rose, when I knew her, had been widowed for several years, living on the remnants of what her once successful husband had bequeathed. My father and Max supplemented Rose's income until her death.

My paternal grandfather, Samuel, for whom I am named, emigrated from Europe to Canada, where he plied his trade as a mediocre and unsuccessful jeweler. There is not one picture of him, nor can I recall my father ever mentioning him.

I always suspected, hoped, that my father, so erudite, so literate and so intelligent, would have left a diary or some sort of history of his life. Gradually, over the years, he shared some stories, but of his arrival in Montreal, at the age of five, from Lodz, Poland (then part of Germany) he said nothing, ever, and surely a bright five-year old would have had memories of those earlier years.

One memory was shared, his Bar Mitzvah, like no other I've ever heard. My father had a part-time job carrying wire from one factory to another. The only detail I have is that he went to the synagogue on Saturday, had his Bar Mitzvah ceremony and then returned to work! I have no knowledge of his preparation for the rite, or who attended. What lingered in his mind was the Dickensian need to return to his job to earn money.

Of my paternal grandfather's parentage, loves, likes, attributes, I know nothing.

My father never mentioned dating, other than the saga of the daughter of a wealthy Orthodox family living in one of those Hudson River Orthodox enclaves, whose parents were intent on arranging their marriage. He expressed some affection for the woman, but knew he could never endure the strict observances and restrictions her religion required (he professed to be an atheist with solely intellectual ties to Judaism) and so he broke off all contact. The only story I know of his courtship of my mother came from her - they met when he was her instructor at Columbia University night school where she was taking two years of Spanish in six months. She always joked that it was easier to marry him than to pass the course (and, indeed, my mother had an atrocious, even non-existent, ear for languages).

He did confide some memories of friends and college, which were happy and safe for him, and several of his college friends were part of his life until he died. He did share that his honeymoon was a weekend at Niagara Falls, narrated without joy, or any emotion at all.

My mother came from a large Boston family. Her grandparents, surname Shoher, emigrated from Germany in the 1870s, and their eleven surviving children (two died of diphtheria on the journey across the Atlantic) were born in America. Her grandmother was a plain, hard working housewife. Her grandfather was an Orthodox rabbi who became head of the Boston Jewish community in later years. In fact, he and his wife were invited to the White House in 1911 to the 25th anniversary celebration of President and Mrs. Taft (I still have the invitation). They did not attend, I suspect due to lack of Kosher kitchen facilities in the executive mansion or, for that matter, the financial wherewithal to undertake the journey.

Neither my mother nor her two sisters ever mentioned their grandparents. In fact, I have formal portrait photographs of them, but don't even know their first names.

My grandmother, Bertha Gordon, seldom mentioned her parents, and never her husband, Bernhard. He came from a prominent Boston family and was, I finally learned, severely bi-polar. They had four children (the only son, William, died shortly after his birth) but then divorced. The genetic horror was inherited by their eldest child, my godmother, my mother's elder sister, my Aunt Florence.

My mother and her sisters spoke only of their mother, who was a major part of our family until she died when I was in college. Everyone adored her and cared for her throughout her lengthy battle with cardiac disease, to which she finally succumbed at age 76. They also revealed rather catty albeit loving anecdotes about their many first cousins and uncles, but never a word about their grandparents, whom they had known.

As for my maternal grandfather, various tales were invented to suit the moment: he had died young, he was still living in Boston, he traveled around the world until his death. In all likelihood, he perished in an asylum or, at least, a very well monitored residence, but there is no record of his death, nor of a burial place. My grandmother rests in my parents' family plot, as do my father's parents.

How could people, living together for sixty-three years, share so little of their own lives? I am well aware of their generation's preference, even reverence, for secrecy, but a few anecdotes about prior romances or family histories would not have been disloyal or unwelcome.

Why did three sisters, like cloistered nuns upholding some sinister vow, choose never to mention their father or grandparents? Were they abused? Was love so withheld that they carried hatred in their hearts for eighty years? Had they been thus trained by my grandmother who, to me, was the saintliest and most loving of women?

Why did my father's father turn him over to aunts to raise? Was it his only choice? I know he had a horrible earlier childhood on the Lower East Side, but his later youth is a blank page to me, although I did learn that he was a top honors pupil at the prestigious Townsend Harris High School and an honors student at City College.

There are only two surviving photographs my father kept from his young years (other than the one of his mother which I destroyed). One is of himself, at the age of four, a bedraggled urchin in a woolen cap, staring suspiciously at the camera. The other was of Dan Murphy, a counselor at the University Settlement, who mentored him and, literally, directed his formative life. My father, a brilliant man who earned his masters in Romance languages at Columbia University, claimed that he would probably have turned to a career of crime if not for Murphy (a fascinating statement and hypothesis in and of itself). Murphy's photograph was on my father's night table until the day he died.

And even if I, as their son, was not to be included in the secrets of their lives, did they even know of each other's? I am not sure of THAT.

The Greens

T HE GREENS WERE ANOTHER FAMILY grafted to ours through marriage. My mother's cousin, Edna Reinherz, whom I loved and called "Shadow" because she and I would write mystery stories together, married Mort Green, a handsome entrepreneur with three brothers, Bill, Shep and Bernie, and a sister, Ethel, unkindly referred to behind her back as "ethyl Ethel" for sound and compelling reasons! She was a harpy-faced, acid-tongued dilettante with a modest facility at the piano, on which she gave sporadic lessons to young students. Her primary means of survival was the stock market, brilliantly maneuvered by her lover, one of Wall Street's legitimate icons of the early '30s through the '50s.

The most distinguished member of this add-on group was Doctor Isadore Hirschfeld, one of the founders of the field of periodontics. He had the most fscinating collection of toothpicks from across the centuries that one could ever hope to see, including one belonging to Louis XIV of France.

For years, I believed that Doc Hirschfeld was married to a man named Paul, because that was his wife Pauline's nickname.

But I digress. Uncle Morty had several businesses, the most impressive (to me) being Deauville Ice Cream, a sinfully creamy treat. Early on, he had developed a minor heart condition and they moved from their apartment on Washington Square in New York to Key Biscayne to take advantage of the more felicitous Florida climate.

While enjoying the Florida lifestyle, Uncle Morty also had taken on a new mistress (not his first), an Italian whom he set up in a small house down the block from his.

When I was fifteen and obscenely obese, my mother and I visited Edna and Morty. I was not a happy teenager, and even two years of Dexadrine and Benzadrine regimens had failed to help me shed those embarrassing pounds. Uncle Morty saw me in my bathing suit and, giving me a serious appraising look, and with no regard for my feelings (or perhaps he presciently did) proclaimed, "You look like a fucking elephant!"

Time stopped, I felt the blood rush to my head from genuine mortification, and I fled from his presence. But Uncle Morty did for me what all of the pharmaceuticals and doctors could not - he shamed me into losing that weight. In the subsequent six months, I lost 65 pounds, and have never, despite periodic weight fluctuations, approached a similar poundage.

Even at the housewarming for Rose Bell and Bill Green's new home, where the buffet was astonishing, I stuck to fruit and had none of the tempting desserts displayed.

Shep Green was another story, entirely. I don't know (never did know) what he did for a living, but it was suspected that his livelihood was, at best, shady. He was married to a very large and heavy woman named Amy, who had a pet dachshund that she was never without. We didn't see them frequently, but one time we were all at a restaurant in New Jersey (where Morty,

Bill and Shep lived) and Amy, of course, had her dog with her. The animal sat patiently halfway under the table.

A server approached with a tray full of our dinner plates and Aunt Edna claimed she saw Amy's foot fly swiftly out, tripping the poor waiter, and sending all of the food onto the restaurant floor. In a flash, the dog was out, indiscriminately devouring whatever victuals were nearest to him. I remember having to re-order and waiting, quite hungry, for replacement meals to be served.

When Uncle Morty died, there was a large family turnout for the funeral, and, of course, his brother, Bill, and his wife, Rose Bell Green, a tart-tongued Southerner, attended. Obviously, and tactfully, the favored Italian mistress had absented herself from the occasion.

When Aunt Edna and her two sons entered the chapel to take their seats in the front pew, Rose Bell exclaimed, in a sotto voce that could be heard in the parking lot, "I see the wrong widow came, today." A collective gasp filled the sanctuary.

What could have possessed that foul tongued woman even to contemplate such a cruel explosion, such a needless coda to an already heartbreaking scene? For all of the infidelities, Morty and Edna had had a good marriage and Edna loved him deeply. I have no knowledge of any simmering hostilities between the two women that might have prompted that vicious outburst. But vicious it was, and Edna and Rose Bell never spoke or saw one another again. If Rose thought her remark amusing, she missed the mark by a long shot and was shunned by the Greens for the rest of her life. She died shortly after in her 70s; my dear Aunt Edna lingered on, in perfect mental health, until age101!

Slow Fade, Dissolve

PART ONE

I WAS WATCHING MY FATHER-IN-LAW DISAPPEAR. We had never liked one another, so I suspect I was deriving a modest degree of pleasure from his decline.

But my overriding reaction was sorrow and fear – sorrow for what he had become and fear that I might one day be in the same situation. He suffered from macular degeneration and had been diagnosed with FTD, frontal temporal dementia, literally a shriveling of the brain. It is irreversible and incurable (a post mortem diagnosis suggested Lewy Body dementia but let's not be Jesuitical about this - the man was dissolving before our eyes).

I was dealing with a brilliant physician, now like a child or, worse, a nasty moron. He had everything – charm, inordinate good looks, a gregarious public persona, an outwardly loving family and material success. He had practiced obstetrics and gynecology for sixty-six years, until he was ninety-two, delivering over eight thousand babies, and treating the ordinary and the famous with the same caring expertise. He was universally acknowledged as an extraordinary clinician.

To his patients, he was a god and he reveled in his deification. Humility was never his strong suit, and his entire world revolved around, and was defined by, his career. All other aspects of his life took a back seat, including his wife and his three children.

Now I watched this former medical icon shuffle with his cane from room to room. He refused to use either a walker or a hearing aid, because his vanity would not allow these overt signs of decay. He ate breakfast, napped until cocktail time, when he drank too much and fell into a somnolent stupor. Dinner was over by seven, and he went to bed. He rarely spoke, and when he did it was generally irrelevant to what was being discussed, and any conversation was interrupted too frequently by his queries of "Where am I? What did you say?"

The aide who was hired to care for my mother-in-law now spent more time with my father-in-law, walking him to the table or the couch or the bed. This man, who was so fastidious about his appearance and his clothing, was now soiled and wrinkled; he smelled sour, and his sparse hair was unkempt, even after combing. He was perpetually chilled to the bone, and wore two sweaters and still complained of the cold. He was most comfortable in his home up north, where the temperature was maintained at a sweat-inducing ninety degrees for his comfort – everything was always for his comfort above all else.

His children, while they loved him, were appalled at his callous and sadistic treatment of people, generally weaker individuals who could not stand up to him. The nurses in his office were frightened of him. He was a bully. Thoughtless and inconsiderate, he indulged his hedonistic urges, oblivious to the pain he caused.

As I sat silently watching the shell of this human being, I could only feel pity for him, simultaneously focusing on the pain he was now inadvertently causing others in different ways. His wife, unable to maneuver without her own walker, attended him at meals, cutting his food, even feeding him. At one dinner at our home, he began eating ice cream with his fingers. He was now inconsistent in his actions, generating a perpetual alert as to what he might suddenly do.

The man was now ninety-four. Given his family genes, he could conceivably carry on for several more years (his aunt and uncles lived into their late nineties, in perfect physical and mental health).

"It's breaking my heart," said my mother-in-law, seeing her former Adonis, her husband of sixty-seven years, turning into a garden slug. "He's lived too long," said my wife and her brother, who earnestly prayed that he be the first to die.

We had moved my in-laws to their Florida home permanently. The change was almost unnoticed by him, but my mother-in-law, desperate to be independent again (though she never could be, having suffered two strokes and a heart attack) kept talking about returning north to their home of fifty-four years (empty now, and on the market). She also was convinced that she would drive again, one day. We said nothing. Her physical therapist took her for a driving test, but she would never even be able to get into the car herself, much less pack her walker and operate a vehicle. We left her car up north for a granddaughter to use.

We tried to be considerate and solicitous of these two aging people. We had them to our home for dinners, we took them to restaurants and the theater (a complex and tedious ordeal). Both of them, who had been so positive and appreciative of life, had turned negative. My mother-in-law now complained about everything and everybody. My father-in-law cared about nothing except his afternoon drinks. Happily, many of his nasty, misanthropic instincts had retreated into the pablum of his brain.

The outcome of this dilemma, this drama, was obvious. But waiting for it was debilitating and sorrowful. Several years before, my in-laws had told us of their personal pact to commit suicide in tandem when they both felt that life was no longer worthwhile. They had all the necessary ingredients stored at home ready for that rather Wagnerian exit. Ironically, the time for such decision making eluded my father-in-law, so we now merely waited and waited, not for Dr. Kevorkian, but for Mother Nature, to end it.

PART TWO

My father-in-law finally, mercifully, died. On December 26th of 2009, we'd given him a 95th birthday dinner party at a local restaurant, secluded in a private room where other patrons could not see him eat with his fingers, or watch him try to spoon the one candle on the birthday cake my son-in-law had baked for the occasion.

His dementia had steadily worsened over the past year, so my wife decided we should stage this celebration while he could, at least, attend.

There is a photograph of him at that dinner with my two children in which he reveals that idiot grin peculiar to the demented – eyes unfocused and a wide smile trained on nothing at all. It is like those horrid pictures of pet dogs dressed up in clown costumes for a party in the 1920's – they look grotesque and, however silly, also frightening.

I said to my wife, "He'll be gone in 30 days." She didn't agree, citing to me the statistics that many people in his condition lived on for years.

In January, the old man was hospitalized; he could no longer eat because his esophagus was paralyzed. They inserted a feeding shunt into his stomach, which he pulled out within 24 hours. I tried to picture that particularly bloody effort in my mind, but could not. How big was the hole? What total damage was inflicted? How much did it hurt? Could he even feel it?

We spent days at the hospital watching him deteriorate, listening to his moans and irrational complaints, repeated angrily and endlessly. He struck out at phantom enemies in the air, returning occasionally to lucidity and conversing with those of us in his room.

I sat there frozen, feeling nothing but wrath over the way this man had treated me for forty-four years. I had allowed him to rent space in my head and now, the lease was expiring and I was shortly to be freed.

Within a week he was moved to hospice, where the primary aim was to facilitate a painless and rapid death.

Even though wrapped in his clean diaper, he yelled that he needed to use the bathroom. The hospice nurses actually took him to the toilet where nothing happened, and he returned to bed, complaining, again, of his need to use the toilet. They treated him as though he were the sanest of men; they were the saintliest of caregivers.

He could not be given food or drink for fear of aspiration, so the treatment of choice was morphine, which allowed him to starve to death without pain.

My mother-in-law, infirm and on a walker, leaned on the bed railing and stroked his face and arm. Occasionally, he called her name; "Lucy! Lucy! I'm not happy." She wept and told him he would be home, again, soon.

I sat there during my hours of vigil, as resentful as ever of this dying specter, holding my tongue because my resentments were mine alone, and not to be shared with anyone, certainly not at this sensitive time. When he called my name, I did not answer, pretending – assuming – that he was having more hallucinations. No one questioned my behavior. At this point, appropriately, I was merely background noise.

I replayed those forty-four years over and over; it was the movie, "Ground Hog Day" and I could not get beyond a certain point, at which moment the film began again.

It was at the beginning of a Board meeting I attended that my daughter called, on January 25th, to say that her grandfather was dead. She was the only family member at hospice at that moment.

I drove to meet her and we waited in the lobby for my wife and mother-in-law to arrive. My brother-in-law had already flown in from New Hampshire. We all gathered at the bedside to be with the corpse. The Hospice personnel advised us that there was no rush – we could spend up to three hours with the body, after which the unpleasant throes of decomposition, decay and rigor mortis would begin in earnest.

I watched almost in horror as my mother-in-law patted her deceased husband's head and cried, "Lou, how could you leave me like this?" She kissed that cold, unlined, waxy cheek.

My wife didn't cry, nor did my daughter. Perhaps they had anticipated this moment for so long that they had internally bid farewell weeks, even months, before.

After an hour or so, we agreed to leave and let the funeral home attend to the body. Preparations had already been made for burial and a crypt purchased. The rest of the out-of-town family arrived in short order.

The service at the crypt was short and dignified. Our muffled conversations while waiting for the rabbi echoed through the marble corridors. My mother-in-law sat bolt upright, staring at the coffin at the front of our small gathering. My wife had arranged for everyone in the family to have a white rose to place on the casket and say a few words. I was unprepared for this ritual, and when my turn came, I could only say, "You had a great run. Godspeed on the next one." It wasn't what my heart wanted to say – still, no one blanched.

I'm not sure that anyone even heard me. It didn't matter.

Shoe Shine

My father owned seventy-seven pairs of custom-made shoes from Peale in London. My mother often voiced semi-humorous regret that he, not she, was the fashion plate in the family.

In the fall of 1958, after college, I was living at home with my family, a daytime student at Columbia University Graduate School of Business. My parents, rather suddenly, decided they were going on a trip around the world and would be gone for three months.

I wanted to do something for my father, either to please him or win his favor - I'm not certain - but my gift brainstorm was to have all of his shoes shined for his return (other than the ones he took on their journey). Ask me why and I'd have to consult the entire staff at Payne-Whitney.

My father was a cultivated sybarite; he spoke five languages and had a master's in Romance Languages from Columbia University. His love of luxury was particularly conspicuous when it came to clothes. He had eighteen overcoats, twelve hats, innumerable Wetzel custom-made suits, and shirts and underwear made in Paris. After he died, we found unopened boxes of shirts from his French shirt maker. But ah, those seventy-seven pairs of shoes. (Ultimately, at the suggestion of his good friend, Max Gordon, the Broadway producer, we donated all of his clothing, including the shoes, to the Actor's Fund, hoping that some slim, indigent thespians could take advantage of the windfall of luxurious size 7B custom-made footgear) and extraordinarily fine and expensive clothing, even including two dozen brand new French shirts.

On Broadway and 73rd street, in front of the Chase National Bank, were two young black brothers who ran a little shoe shine stand. I explained that I wanted them to come to our apartment and shine my father's shoes on a Sunday, when the maid was off.

We agreed on a price of fifty-cents a pair and the boys were to arrive on Sunday morning. I removed all of the shoes from the mahogany shoe racks in my father's closet, and laid them out neatly on newspaper on the kitchen floor. Each pair had its own mahogany brass-handled shoe trees; the floor looked like the terra cotta soldiers in Xian.

Sunday morning, at exactly the appointed hour, the boys arrived at the service entrance. They walked the short hallway into the kitchen, stared at the shoes on the floor and asked, "How many fathers you got?" I knew I had the right kids!

Hours later, they finished and I gave them each five dollars extra (a goodly sum in 1958), showed them out and put the shoes back in the closet.

They had done a wonderful job. The fine soft leathers glowed with their deep, rich polish, and his closet had the aroma of a new Ferrari.

When my parents came home, I waited for my father to choose a pair of shoes to wear. He noticed the fine luster and I told him what I'd done. It was one of the few gifts I ever gave him that elicited gratitude and genuine pleasure.

Never again did I give him any present which remotely approached his appreciation of that mass shoe shine. Our relationship see-sawed over the years, distilling an unsettling combination of warmth, cruelty, mutual admiration, mistrust, and love.

I marvel at the inadvertent perspicacity of those two young brothers, innocently asking, "How many fathers you got?"

The "Steps"

MY PATERNAL GRANDFATHER, SAMUEL KATES, remarried after the death of his first wife, Hinda. My impression of the man (whom I never met) was that he had a fetish for homely women. I conclude that because his first wife (at least in the one photograph of her) was hideous.

Grandma Kates, his second wife, who outlived him by many years, was a squat, unkempt crone with three daughters, my father's step-sisters. Her two natural daughters were, far and away, the ugliest women I've ever seen. Her third daughter, Janet, she had adopted and Janet, in a plain way, was almost attractive. Rose and Janet were good people, somehow sidelined by life, but they were warm and kind to me.

Grandma Kates was originally married to a man named Brown, which was the surname of her three girls, whom my mother conveniently christened, "The Steps."

Rose, the eldest, was tall and thick, with an oversized, squarish head topped by inky black dyed hair worn in no particularly known style. Her small, beady black eyes were too close together and she had thin, black penciled eyebrows and no eyelashes, so one got the impression of being face to face with a rather unintelligent Tasmanian devil.

Sally, the middle sister, was equally homely and tall, a mannish woman with thick glasses and an acid tongue - an ugly harpy, mean, surly, insulting and smug. Her venom was directed solely at Rose; both sisters were caring and cosseting to little Janet. One can only imagine what Mr. Brown looked like, given these progeny who probably combined the features of both of their parents.

They lived in a cramped apartment in Brighton Beach, Brooklyn. It was rumored that their mother stored live fish in the one bathtub until it was time to slaughter and prepare them for gefilte fish for Passover.

Rose and Sally both worked in Manhattan, enduring the hour-long subway rides to and from home. I think their work was secretarial - in any event, neither had climbed any occupational ladder of note, but they earned enough to subsist in that dreadful and dreary apartment.

Janet had several positions in retailing including one lengthy stint in sales at Georg Jensen on Fifth Avenue. Her final job was at Cartier's, where she was put in charge of customer relations, and given an alias along the lines of "Jean Dawn" or some such, ostensibly to put her on a supposed par with the Cartier clientele. Janet was patient and relatively articulate, certainly not of the class one would suspect as being a Cartier customer, but she was successful at her job and was well liked by her superiors and her clientele.

These pathetic women totally lacked social graces, education or charm or even friends. They existed in their ugly Brighton Beach apartment like characters from a Chekov play, without benefit of funds or servants. They were, apart from my mother, totally alone in the world

My mother always kept in touch with my father's family, both the impecunious "Steps" and my father's very wealthy extended family in Brooklyn.

We had semi-annual visits with The Steps, always at our home because I think my parents were embarrassed to be seen in public with such unattractive companions.

They also attended my Bar Mitzvah, giving me a gold signet pinky ring which I'd always wanted. Happily, my mother selected the ring according to her taste and was reimbursed by the three women.

We had more contact with Janet, whom my father more or less took under his wing to try and expose her to literature, while my mother worked on manners and wardrobe options.

It was Janet who provided me access to the diamond merchant whom Cartier's used for their jewelry to purchase my wife's engagement ring.

The last time I saw The Steps was at my son David's Bar Mitzvah in 1982, to which they had duly taken the subway from Brighton Beach to Grand Central Station, the train to Larchmont, and then a cab to the Larchmont Temple.

Out of both kindness and embarrassment, I seated them at my table, where they had absolutely nothing to say. It was difficult, but I felt that I was, in some way, doing something for my father he would have appreciated. At the time, my mother was deep in the grip of dementia, in her apartment with her aide, unable to attend the festivities for her grandson.

I assume all three Steps have died. I was never notified of any of their demises, nor did I ever contact them after the Bar Mitzvah. Lives change, priorities morph, but memories linger.

If Wishes Were Horses

MY GRANDMOTHER'S ELDEST BROTHER, MY great-uncle Louie, was not a bright man. He might charitably have been characterized as a plodder. Of the five brothers and six sisters who survived diphtheria in his family, it was the boys who lacked the spark and imagination for achieving financial success. On the other hand, in an ironic genetic twist of fate, all of the six women were extremely successful, either by reason of their wits and talents, or by the directions and business acumen they provided for their husbands' enterprises.

Also, they all had great legs.

Louie married early, had three children, was widowed young and lived to 91. I don't know what he did for a living in New York, but early in the twentieth century, he met Marcus Loew. They became fast friends and ardent pinochle playing buddies

One day, Loew came to Uncle Louie with a business proposition. He was investing in movie theaters, which, he said, would become very profitable. The film industry was dawning, and Loew saw this as the road to fortune. Would Louie put in $10,000 and become a partner? Uncle Louie had the money, but he gave this much deep thought, and justified his ultimate refusal with the rationale that no sane person would spend a Saturday afternoon in a dark room watching pictures on a wall, even ones that moved, when he could be out in the park or at the beach. This was typical of the corporate farsightedness of my uncle and, probably, his brothers, as well, and thus was a major family fortune capitulated.

I had heard this story many times across family dinner tables, and it was always told with a slight snicker and a rueful sigh of resignation. But my teenage imagination ran riot with the fiction of Uncle Louie having been shrewder and actually becoming a co-founder of Loew's, and thus an owner of Metro-Goldwyn-Mayer studios.

In my adolescent fantasy, I would have been S. Gordon Kates, boy Hollywood tycoon, a nepotistic triumph, producing major films, exhausted from fighting off eager starlets, cosseted and embarrassingly well paid for life. I could have been the successor to Irving Thalberg! Of course, all of that was twenty years before I was even born.

Also, it never dawned on me for a moment that I totally lacked the compulsive venality imperative for survival in the film industry. I just knew about the glamour and the money, and it was a heady fantasy.

But, if Marcus Loew had befriended my grandmother, instead...or even married her; now THERE is a fantasy worth conjuring.

All In The Genes

I ENJOY UNTANGLING THE TENTACLES OF extended family relationships acquired through marriages or other more sordid invocations. One such relationship involved Minnie Pearlstein Nechamkis - yes, that was her real name, married to Mike Nechamkis.

My grandmother's sister, Celia, had married Meyer Pearlstein, a wealthy merchant in New York, whose sister was "Aunt" Minnie. I have the profile photograph of Aunt Celia, a patrician woman with a Roman nose, upswept hair, and a high lace collar, closely resembling Edith Wharton. She and Meyer were childless, one of three of my grandmother's eleven surviving siblings who bore no heirs. We still have a sapphire and diamond bar pin that Celia left to my grandmother.

Aunt Celia died prematurely of encephalitis in the 1920's, but my mother always kept in touch with Minnie and her daughter, Dora Berson, a critic for a now defunct classical music trade magazine.

Minnie was a sweet person, mousy and rather quiet, although she and my grandmother, relatives only by marriage, were fairly close and enjoyed leisurely afternoons in our apartment.

After tea and cakes and cookies, Minnie would excuse herself and head to the bathroom, where, legend has it, she stuck her finger down her throat and puked - possibly, probably anorexia nervosa! No wonder she was thin to the point of emaciation.

Her daughter Dora, on the other hand, was a breathtaking, natural red-haired beauty, with a beguiling, throaty voice and a vibrant personality who could converse intelligently about almost any subject with acumen and humor. I think that, as a young boy, I was in love with Dora, who'd had the good fortune to marry a man named Harold Berson, thus escaping her maiden name of Nechamkis, retaining Berson even after Harold and she divorced.

I would confide to my mother and grandmother how frighteningly homely Aunt Minnie was, to which they both responded with detailed descriptions of what a great beauty Minnie had been when young - in fact, Dora, they said, was the image of her mother! Impossible, I thought.

The years passed on and Aunt Minnie died, but Dora, who loved our family, continued to visit, even after my grandmother had also passed away. And with each visit, I could notice the slight changes - red hair a bit less vibrant, smile lines that hadn't previously been visible, and a somewhat stooped posture where, before, she had been ramrod straight. She didn't inherit her mother's anorexia, but with each visit, she looked more and more like her.

At the final visits, before Dora herself died, she was the image of Aunt Minnie - bowed over, thin as a rail, drooping nose which once had been Roman in its elegance, and claw-like hands, which previously had played a pretty impressive piano. The transformation, stunning and inconceivable, was complete. I wish I could have had one of those stop-motion films of Dora's appearance, year by year, to document the incontrovertible truth of her morphing into her mother. and I finally had to believe the stories I'd been told earlier about Aunt Minnie.

Aunt Jenny

I ACKNOWLEDGE THAT THERE'S CHEAP AND then there's cheap, but my great aunt Jenny and her husband, Charlie Cohen, elevated parsimony to an art form. Whether due to an innate German stinginess, or just plain meanness, we'll never know.

In the 1920s, Charlie, a well-to-do gentleman, bought a new Cadillac. He and Jenny took it out every Sunday for an eight-mile drive, and then headed home, having used up his agreed-upon gas ration for the week The car remained in the garage until the following Sunday (I assume that when there were rains or snowstorms on Sundays in Boston – for which Charlie may even have prayed - he saved even more money).

Aunt Jenny was one of my grandmother's siblings, whom I only knew as a plain elderly woman. She had married Charlie, a Boston investor with whom she shared twenty-something happy, childless years; Charlie died in the late 30s when Jenny was still fairly young, and while his will left her everything, no one knew where everything (or anything) was.

It was only when Jenny decided some repairs were needed to her house that some pleasant surprises awaited her. When the door frame of one room was loosened, out fell several bankbooks, reflecting hefty cash deposits. Being fairly intelligent, Jenny had the workmen loosen some other lintels, and more books were discovered. At the end, having profitably investigated every lintel in her home, Jenny emerged a rather financially comfortable woman, but she was as compulsively cheap as Charlie had been, although less inventively secretive.

Aunt Jenny paid periodic visits to New York to visit my grandmother, who lived with us. As she proudly announced, in her clipped Boston accent, "My neighbors say it's not polite to visit relatives for less than two weeks." So, year after year, she graciously accepted her neighbors' generous advice, and spent four weeks with us, two in the winter, when she took the train from Boston, and at least two in the summer, when we were in the country, and she and her brother, Uncle Bob and his common-law wife, Sally Aaron, drove to Connecticut.

When I was fifteen, in 1951, Aunt Jenny visited us for her winter fortnight, and my parents, for some reason, were away for one weekend. My grandmother was not well enough to go out, so Aunt Jenny magnanimously announced that she was going to take me out to lunch that Saturday.

The heavens didn't quite move, but it was a startling invitation. Soon, however, I learned its limitations. Aunt Jenny was taking me to Woolworth's Five-and-Ten at Broadway and 79th street where they still had a lunch counter.

Jenny was broad, with a large head resulting from Paget's disease, with sparse reddish hair that one could see through to her scalp. Her dark rimmed glasses neither enhanced nor detracted from her essentially homely looks, and she wore no cosmetics to enhance or conceal her sharp and unattractive features, including a perpetually hypertensive roseate complexion. For all the years I knew her, she looked as though she had a bad case of the measles. Her clothing was uninspired wool, suitable for Boston winters during the 1930s, but, even to my fifteen-year old eyes, rather ugly, and I was embarrassed to be seen with her.

Still, we walked the five blocks to Woolworth's and sat down at the counter and read the menu.

"What'll you have?" asked Aunt Jenny, and I, having found only one remotely acceptable item, replied, "A turkey sandwich on white toast."

"My Gawd," she exclaimed, "That's the most expensive thing on the menu!" Her ruddy complexion seemed to pale even as she spoke.

"There's nothing else I like," I explained. I think the price was around one dollar, maybe a dollar and twenty-five cents.

She studied me for a moment, and then announced, "In that case, we're leaving," and she slipped off her stool and headed for the door. I had no choice but to follow. We walked back to my apartment at a brisk pace, not speaking. When we arrived home, my grandmother asked me how lunch was, and I told her what had happened. She sort of rolled her eyes, knowing her sister, and our maid made us some tuna fish sandwiches.

From my vantage point, my great aunt had gotten some exercise and saved about three dollars in the bargain. Whoever said there's no such thing as a free lunch had yet to meet Aunt Jenny.

But Jenny was not the only member of that family who had raised mooching to new heights. Of my grandmother's many siblings, she was closest to Jenny and her brother Bob, the youngest in her family. Bob and Sally lived in Worcester, close to Aunt Jenny. No matter the decline and decay of their once genteel neighborhood, they all stayed on in those homes until their deaths.

Bob had found a perfect, thought-free career for himself, after success on the stage had eluded him. I was always aware of the similarity of Bob's life with that of "The Jazz Singer," the first talking movie - son of a rabbi goes into show business, but this one, unlike Al Jolson, failed !

Bob worked in the stockroom at Sears, Roebuck, a position undoubtedly suitable for his intellectual level, amassing a small fortune in Sears stock over the years.

Sally, a milliner for a prominent Boston couture salon, had lived with Bob for over thirty years, all the while professing herself to be a virgin. Well, I would think to myself, why not? It had been done before! When she and Bob traveled, it was always separate rooms, so perhaps her claim was valid. And I always had my suspicions about him - he had a slight lisp, a sure giveaway to a young mind in the 1950s.

Every summer Bob, Sally and Jenny would visit us at our summer home, never for less than a two-week stay. They brought nothing but their personalities and insatiable appetites as house gifts, although some years Sally offered a hat or a veil for my mother.

Because of the Bob and Sally sleeping requirements, Uncle Bob would share my room, while Sally and Aunt Jenny shared a guest room (and would that I could have been a fly on that wall!).

My mother and our maid, also named Sally, prepared large, elaborate meals for our guests — three a day plus afternoon snacks. My grandmother had to rest some time during the day, my father was in the city during the week (crafty and lucky, I always thought), so my mother and I were the diversion for the proper Bostonians.

Providing entertainment was not difficult - our guests ate and slept, ate and slept. It was something at which they were extraordinarily proficient, and they never demanded any sort of outside activity to relieve the languorous and stomach stretching monotony of their days in the sun.

Bob would spin tales of his youth, especially his days on the stage. Sometimes, he even performed routines he'd mastered in his vaudeville days. Sally, outside the zone of early family recollections, would doze like the dormouse in Alice in Wonderland, occasionally waking to re-enter whatever was being discussed. It was deadly dull, but my mother had loved her uncle as a young girl. When he would visit her childhood home, Uncle Bob would scrunch himself into the dumbwaiter and leap out at her and her sisters to frighten them; they loved him for his childish antics and recitations of his days on the regional stage.

The fortnight visit gradually drew to a close. The Bostonians packed their bags, and descended for breakfast, after which they eased into armchairs to digest the meal before washing up for lunch and the drive home.

Every year, without fail, my mother prepared gargantuan food packages for the relatives to take home, her civilian version of the Marshall Plan. A large brisket and a couple of roast chickens were wrapped, along with various side dishes and cakes and cookies. "Much too much, for Gawd's sake!" exclaimed Sally, as she stuffed her pelf into some shopping bags. Aunt Jenny didn't even bother to protest as she stowed her victuals for the drive back to Worcester.

Uncle Bob put the various bags into the car trunk, and returned to the house, where we all sat down to a large lunch.

It was time for the departure. We gathered in the driveway, hugging and kissing goodbye, and assuring one another we were looking forward to the next summer visit. I knew they would be back, having hibernated all winter on the provisions my mother had provided.

Once my grandmother had died, we gave up summer homes and the visits ceased. Jenny and Sally died without our ever seeing them again. My mother subsequently became the conservator of Uncle Bob's estate to protect it from her predatory cousins who all hoped for a slice of the considerable pie.

After Uncle Bob's death, we learned that my mother and her elder sister, Florence, were Uncle Bob's sole heirs. In that stultifying, unchallenging stock-room career, Bob had amassed a modest fortune in Sears, Roebuck stock and, given his familial parsimony, he had also saved a fair amount of cash. In due course, the legacy fell to me.

I can attest to the fact that the inheritance was put to good use.

September Shocker!

I OFTEN THINK OF THE BIZARRE turn of fate befalling my friend, Bob Rubin.

Bob and I attended The Fieldston School, he on a full scholarship. Our small class of 77 was like a family, with all of its attractions, affections, dysfunctions and teenage angst. But Bob was special, which everyone knew. I was fortunate to count him as a friend.

He was very smart and very shy. Tall and lanky, he moved awkwardly, as though connected by wires. His skin was the color of stale mustard, and he had thick lips that he continually licked to keep them moist.

Bob sported thick, horn-rimmed glasses, which made him look so studious that he was nicknamed "Horace."

He lived three blocks from me, and we would take the forty minute subway ride to school together almost every day. We shared a lot on those rides up to and back from Riverdale; we communicated easily without fear of judgment or criticism - we were good friends!

The routine was always the same. I arrived at his drab apartment on Amsterdam Avenue and his mother answered the door. Mrs. Rubin released the door chain and let me in.

The apartment smelled of toast and stale bed linens. "Want anything?" she would ask, and I would reply that I had already had breakfast. She was short, with olive skin and gray hair that always seemed to be tangled and greasy.

"Bobby," she would call, "Bobby, get ready! Don't forget your books." Mrs. Rubin had a desperation in her voice, as though responding to a taunt. She fidgeted, always fussing, nervous, ungrounded, somehow. Mr. Rubin sat at their kitchen table, reading the New York <u>Times,</u> and pretty much ignoring Mrs. Rubin. A radio was always playing classical music from WQXR.

It took about five minutes for Bob to get his things together and be ready to leave. I stood awkwardly in their little hall, taking in the threadbare furnishings of their home, and the cramped small rooms in which the three of them lived. My home was large and spacious, and I was uncomfortable in those dark and dingy surroundings.

In the spring of 1954, we were seniors, and Bob had been accepted to Harvard on a full scholarship, and was going to spend the summer in Holland.

It was only when classes began in September that we learned what happened. Bob's father died suddenly of a heart attack in early August. Mrs. Rubin called Bob to return to New York at once. Bob, flying home for his father's funeral, was on a KLM airliner that crashed into the Atlantic. No one survived, and they never recovered his body.

Suddenly, catastrophically alone and unable to cope with her double disaster, three weeks later, Mrs. Rubin hanged herself from her kitchen chandelier.

If Music Be The Food Of Love

"HEDY SPIELTER," SAID MY MOTHER, and she might as well have clubbed me with a mallet! Hedy Spielter ran the music school that I attended from age 4 to 12. I hated Hedy Spielter as a child and 47 years later, I hated her. 69 years later, I still hate her.

I had arrived for my weekly visit to mother's Fifth Avenue apartment where she gradually, and inexorably, slid towards total mental incapacity and death. The onset of her dementia came shortly after my father's death the year before, and the severity was increasing. I refused to put her into a nursing home, so I maintained her in the apartment with her maid plus a 24/7 aide whose weekend replacements stole almost all of her jewelry. My cousin had warned me about these caregivers, but I ignored her, thinking that when my mother would want a piece to wear, it would be there for her. Almost nothing of value was left.

I came every Friday to pay both women. On this particular morning, my mother, now 82, seemed to recognize me, and said, "I'm going to take piano lessons." I gasped.

"But you don't have a piano anymore" I said. "I'll buy one," she replied. "From whom will you take these lessons?" I asked. "Hedy Spielter," she said.

The Institute for Modern Piano Technique was housed in an ornate, town house on West 79th street in Manhattan. Spielter was the titular head and also the driving force, a respected piano instructor. Also in residence were her old German mother and her alcoholic brother, "Uncle Willie" who roamed the rooms, drink in hand, cigarette dangling from his alcohol-swollen lips, overseeing student practice sessions. In earlier, healthier days, he had been a modestly successful pianist and transcriber. His barroom alcohol stench was a constant presence in the dim hallways and practice rooms.

And then there was Monsieur Eppele - Jules was his name - a three hundred pound French Jew, Hedy's long time lover. To this day, just imagining their sexual congress defies reality, much less gravity. They occupied the entire third floor of the house, which consisted of huge his and her bedrooms, each roomy enough to house a baby grand piano, used by the students. These bedrooms were divided by the spacious washroom/bathroom they shared.

Eppele was a dilettante musician with a good sense of humor who clearly played second fiddle to his mistress, whom he probably considered svelte. And in her youth, Hedy may have been. On the wall of the staircase leading to the premier floor was a shoulder-length profile portrait of Hedy, lean, still watery-blue eyed, with a swan-like neck, her ski nose tilted slightly upward, a Teutonic Circe from the 1920s.

I recall one snowy evening when I was to be picked up by my mother at the school. Eppele was displaying his agglomeration of impossibly rococo clocks and miniatures. When my mother arrived, the two of them spent at least an hour examining and savoring this assortment of European craftsmanship, both being ardent collectors of antiques. I saw a different side of Eppele that evening - gregarious and friendly.

Spielter knew her music, but she was an innately German teacher of the old school, intolerant of error, unfeeling towards children. When someone made a mistake, she cracked their hands down on the keys, crying out, "Shmeer! Schmeer!" (mistake, sloppy). She would frequently administer a moderate cuff to the side of one's head when some playing displeased her.

The best thing about the school was that house, a French rococo building typical of its 1910 era style, solid, luxurious, impressive and creepy.

The ground floor entry began with an enormous foyer with a large fireplace. Beyond it was a very large dining room which the Spielter family used; when it was a private residence, this was the servant's eating place. Beyond it was a tremendous kitchen facing the small back yard, with appliances that probably dated to the house's origin. Old lady Spielter, tiny, with thin white hair trussed into a bun at her neck, did all of the cooking in that antique scullery.

The second floor, the "salon" floor had, at the house's front, a very large living room with a bowed window, in which sat two concert grand pianos, used only by the most promising students when they were preparing for a concert.

The central "reception" area at the head of the staircase, was furnished with reproduction French antique furniture, a bronze statue of Mozart playing a violin, an upright piano and a mammoth marble fireplace. To the right was the formal dining room, also with a fireplace at one end, and tall stained glass windows. Under the window was a long marble-topped table on which students practiced "driving nails," a regimen of pounding one's fingertips against the stone to strengthen the fingers. There was also another upright piano.

Just beyond the dining room was the service staircase off a pantry containing the dumb waiter, in which meals were originally transported from the kitchen below to the servants to bring to the dining table.

The fourth floor consisted of several fairly small rooms which had probably been children's bedrooms when the home was new. Each contained an upright piano and those were where we students practiced.

Finally, there was the fifth floor, with a skylight above the narrow stairs, and a warren of smaller windowless rooms, each with retractable skylight, which must have been for the original household staff. These, too, were employed as practice rooms, and each had yet another upright piano.

We twenty or so students attended the school every weekday after school, from 3:00 until five in the afternoon, and some Saturday mornings. Perhaps because of some remote local ordinance, we were given twenty minutes of outside play in the back yard outside the kitchen, a grim concrete rectangle with a swing and one jungle gym.

I was considered a prodigy at the time. Subsequently, I gave several solo recitals in concerts staged by the school, at

Town Hall and Carnegie Recital Hall. I also played one solo concert at Carnegie Hall, proper, and was one of four pianists from the school who performed a Bach four-piano concerto with sixteen members of the New York Philharmonic at that same Carnegie Hall.

One by-product of my musical instruction was my command performances for my parents' dinner guests.

During cocktails, I was trotted out in pajamas and robe to play for their friends. Even at five or six, I sensed how totally uninterested these adults were in my playing, no matter how accomplished. I kept my head down to avoid their condescending glances of boredom or even annoyance. Polite applause, and I was whisked off to bed, while the grownups went in to dine.

I think my father viewed my musical talent as a moderately amusing lagniappe attached to an already gifted son. My mother was clearly the instigator of the lessons, ostensibly because while in my playpen, I would hum tunes that I heard on the radio, and my nurse passed on this intelligence, which started the chain of events.

Music school was not enjoyable. I loved, and will always love, music, but the stress of that overly disciplined and hermetic environment weighed heavily on my young shoulders. The straw that broke the camel's back was to come in the spring before my twelfth birthday.

Alan Mandel and I were close friends at the school, and we enjoyed horsing around when not actually practicing. One day we were wrestling in Monsieur Eppele's bedroom and my loafer flew off my foot and smashed the bowed glass of an antique French curio cabinet. I panicked, terrified at the thought of Miss Spielter's wrath and retaliation, so I swore Alan to the stupid lie that we were horsing around, and the vibrations of the floor broke the glass. A ridiculous fabrication and one that wouldn't even excuse the damage done to that fine piece of furniture. But in panic we do dumb things, and lying seemed, in that panicky moment, preferable to confession and its consequences.

Mandel confessed the truth under Spielter's interrogation. She marched me to the small back pantry behind the dining room. She ordered me to drop my trousers and lean over a chair, whereupon she proceeded to beat me with a hairbrush, crying out, "Liar! Liar! This is what liars get!" I could feel the welts forming and the blood trickling from the impact of the bristles, but I made no sounds. I put back my hands to deflect the blows, but she just hit them as well, drawing blood. Her wrath was finally spent; I pulled up my pants, left the school and walked the six blocks home.

My father was out of town on business. I told my mother what had happened and begged her to call the police and have Spielter arrested, on what charges I couldn't even specify; I just wanted her jailed, even killed. I did not return to the school next day, but when my father came home and heard the story, his sympathies lay with Spielter; he told me I deserved the punishment I'd received for lying. He and she had fairly identical views on corporal punishment for children.

I begged to be removed from the school; I'd had enough and I was terrified of Miss Spielter. But I was not taken from the school roster, so I took matters into my own hands and simply did not show up. I spent my afternoons at my friend Steven Pennoyer's home playing Monopoly, Of course, Hedy

Spielter reported my absence to my parents, and the stage was set for confrontation and my first real act of defiance. I refused to go back, no matter what they did or said, and so my tenure at the school finally ended.

"Hedy Spielter" indeed!

I returned to the moment realizing, heartbreakingly, that the initiation of my music lessons was a manifestation of my mother's unfulfilled dream for herself, a secret desire to learn to play the piano that she held for forty-six years, if not more.

Shame!

WEST 72ND STREET, IN THE 1940s was a remarkable place - The Dakota, Schwartz's Out Of This World Chocolate, and Horn & Hardart's AUTOMAT. Nothing could ever surpass the thrill of dispensing hot cocoa from a gilded dolphin's mouth, or plugging nickels into a slot and having your sandwich miraculously appear from a revolving container.

And if that weren't enough, there was the hot food section, where you got a juicy Salisbury steak and the creamiest mashed potatoes in America, although my cousin Billy preferred the macaroni and cheese.

We went often to that Automat on Thursdays, my mother and I, a sort of night out when the maid was off and my father was at his club enjoying his handball, swim and high stakes gin rummy games.

The large restaurant was populated with assorted families, individuals and several homeless men nursing cups of hot coffee.

On one of those Thursday excursions, when I was about 8 or 9, we sat at our table, enjoying the meal. At an adjacent table sat a young girl, perhaps 12 years old, with her governess.

I immediately noticed that the girls' hand shook violently as she raised her fork to her mouth. And, with an unintentional cruelty, I imitated her shaking, and she noticed it immediately. With a shriek, she got up and ran weeping from the restaurant, closely followed by her attendant.

My mother delivered a powerful slap across my face which stung for hours; it was the only time in my life that she struck me!

"That was the worst thing you've ever done!" she berated me. "It was terrible."

She got up, we left our unfinished food and departed the Automat, I, in shock over having been hit and dismayed at being punished for what I thought to be an innocent bit of mimicry. It had never occurred to me that the girl would notice, or that she might take offense at my extraordinary insensitivity. My mother hardly spoke to me for several days after that. I don't think she ever related the incident to my father, who would have inflicted significantly sterner punishment for my act.

Over the years, I did eat at other Automats, while they still existed, but my mother, from time to time, would go back to the one on 72nd street. There, she would meet the former governess, who confided that her charge was afflicted with Muscular Dystrophy and that she and her family had moved back to their original home in Argentina.

In time, probably months later, the awfulness of what I'd done became a reality for me. I wanted to make amends to the girl for hurting her as I did, but the opportunity had passed. I've lived with this regret for seventy-one years, and shall probably harbor it until my death.

Guillain-Barré Syndrome

As I lay there, trach tube in my neck, respirator tube down my throat, feeding tube down my nose, catheter constantly emptying my bladder into its plastic bag, intravenous fluids steadily dripping into my arm, I remembered, savoring the irony, how it all started, at a dinner party at my home with three doctor friends in attendance.

It was Labor Day of 1992 when my wife, Linda, and I always had friends over to celebrate the holiday. We'd had a great barbecue dinner, plenty to drink and were sitting at the table languidly conversing in that relaxed, close way that friends have. My first reaction was that I'd had too much to drink; I was dizzy and feeling really ill, so much so that I had to excuse myself and go to bed. I slept through the night and awoke with a fever of 104. My normal body temperature generally stays flat at 97 degrees, so I knew this was a serious fever. I suffered sweats and dizziness, alternating between normal and the high fever levels.

Linda drove me to the emergency room where the admitting nurse opined that it was probably the flu, there was a lot of it going around. I felt relief at her diagnosis, assuming that most flus could be readily cured.

The physician on call was a doctor whose offices my wife had been asked to freshen up - Seba Krumholtz, the most compassionate and knowledgeable doctor I have ever met, and a doctor who, through his attention, kindness, thoroughness and knowledge, saved my life. It wasn't easy.

I was subjected to a battery of tests, most of which I slept through. I could barely stay awake, as the fever raged within me. Krumholtz seemed to zero in on my liver, and they did a liver biopsy to check it out. A short young doctor, perhaps fifteen or sixteen years of age, came in to perform the procedure, sporting a long device. I was sufficiently awake to understand what was to be done, and I demurred, but the doctors standing around told me I had no choice. Torso bared, arms above my head, eyes closed in panic, I waited while the child practitioner made a mark on my right side, and then placed the instrument against my flesh. Bing! The spring cartridge had plunged into my liver and come back with a sample, and I had felt nothing. I remember thinking that the kid had a real future in medicine. I hope he did - it was the least painful part of my ultimate experience.

Out of the hospital, Linda and I went to play tennis with another couple. I just stood on the court, immobile - I simply couldn't get my legs to move, much less run.

Back in the hospital, over the next few days, more tests were conducted and it was finally determined that I was in the throes of cytomegalovirus, a nasty and persistent affliction which was the cause of my spiking fevers, muscle aches, fatigue, loss of appetite and general malaise.

Once the spiking fevers had subsided, I was sent home, but the reprieve was short lived. A few days later I woke in the early morning hours seized by horrific shooting, stabbing pains across my back and shoulders, as though I were being electrically zapped.

We went back to the hospital for still more tests - hematologists, neurologists and specialists in tropical and infectious diseases all attended to my tormented body, but no firm diagnosis seemed on the horizon.

Back home once more, with the acute pain attacks gone, I tried to resume a normal life, and it was the season of High Holy Days. We attended a break fast at a friend's home, where my favorite Jewish delicacies were arrayed on the buffet table - smoked salmon, sable, whitefish salad and creamed herring. I filled a plate, took one bite and felt that I was devouring guano. The food tasted vile! I told Linda it was rancid, but she acknowledged that the food was fine, it was my taste buds that were out of whack.

I had arranged a surprise 50th birthday party for Linda in December. It was to be themed to the 50s with a juke box at hand to play the songs of the day. But I was also aware of a new development - my feet were not working properly. They were numb and my walk was slightly halting and off kilter. Somehow, I had a premonition of a lengthy illness and while Linda was in New York for a day, I drove to the juke box company to cancel the order for the party; thankfully, I averted a serious car accident.

Linda arrived back in Florida and Dr. Krumholtz suggested a re-visit with the neurological team. They instructed me to take long walk down the hall in their office, while they stood behind me watching my progress away from them and then back. I vaguely heard the words "Guillain Barré" in their soft-spoken conversation but had no idea what it was. However, I was already aware that my feet were sick and now I was unable to curl my toes upward even though I willed them to do so. There was no response, but still we lacked a conclusive decision as to what was wrong..

Two spinal taps later, the diagnosis of Guillain-Barré Syndrome, a rare autoimmune disease, was confirmed, and I was re-admitted to the Boca Raton Hospital.

My in-laws arrived from New York to "visit" when my physician father-in-law proclaimed flat out that I was simply malingering rather than go back to work. Elizabeth, my daughter, made short and pungent shrift of that thoughtless, even vicious, observation, so typical of the man.

Essentially, the condition destroys the myelin sheath that surrounds nerves so that impulses sent to the nerves in the organs are not received. I was immediately put on a regimen of intravenous immunoglobulin injections as the disease gradually (and rather swiftly) progressed.

I began having vivid, bizarre hallucinations which were incredible - ants forming cursive writings on the walls, dreams of being in an intensive care unit which consisted of a series of white spaces separated by gauzy white curtains, where everyone was wearing gas masks. One recurring nightmare had me at a British colonial desert outpost, from the era of Kipling's Raj, which I entered through a large, round, unlit hall. I heard voices from dark doorways surrounding the hall, but couldn't see the people. I was on top of a table and trying desperately to extricate myself from the table top. I heard a few familiar voices, but never saw the hidden throngs. Later, in my dissociation, I was sitting on a chair at the top of the ceiling, looking down at myself in bed.

Soon thereafter, the paralysis extended to my throat and neck and I required an emergency tracheotomy to sustain my breathing. But even that failed to suffice and I was put on a mechanical respirator which remained my life support for several months. Due to my inability to eat or even swallow, I was fed through a tube running from my nose into my stomach, and a catheter was employed to handle my urine output, which needed to be changed every two days. Also, and perhaps most terrifying - I couldn't speak.

My lifeline to sanity was imperiled. The first of several silent panic attacks occurred when I realized I was unable to call for help. I could not manipulate the call button at the side of the bed, nor could I produce a cry for someone to attend me. I would have to rely on the chance that a passing nurse might notice something wrong with me. My silence was my companion and my curse.

Without the gift of speech, my mind raced faster than normal. Things I wanted to say kept backing up, like water against a dam. Increasingly, I could not bear that backlog of unspoken thoughts and I retreated into sleep to escape.

A regimen of plasmapharesis was prescribed, but since the Boca hospital lacked the equipment, I was taken by ambulance to Jackson Memorial Hospital in Miami and housed in the ward holding gunshot wound victims and other patients suffering neurological traumas.

I lay on my bed receiving no real attention; no one came to give me range of motion exercises to keep some degree of mobility of my muscles. It was Linda who provided range of motion exercises to help prevent my muscles from totally atrophying. No one turned me every few hours, so I developed bedsores.

At Jackson, I was convinced that if I could only get out of the bed, I would be able to walk, and my plan was to gradually inch myself down to the foot of the bed, and then slide my feet to the floor. Linda and the nurses and the doctors all told me that I couldn't walk, but I knew that if I could just reach that bed foot, I would.

Despite my increasing paralysis, I was able to edge my body slightly down the bed, disturbing the respirator and the intravenous connections, so they tied me to the bedrails to prevent any further such movements. My innate claustrophobia took hold, and I panicked at this enforced immobility. But I was too weak to resist, and gave up the futile effort to reach the foot of the bed.

The plasmapharesis treatments were torture. Essentially, a large needle was placed in my vein and the blood was removed, washed in a special machine and then returned to my body. This procedure, painful in itself, took about three hours, and it had to be done for six or seven consecutive days. My veins were collapsing and each needle insertion became more painful. One time a needle broke and they had to switch to the other arm.

Throughout this procedure, the elderly Cuban physician administering the treatment was entertained by two other young doctors who sat opposite my bed, jovially discussing the boats they planned to buy and the homes they planned to build. Despite my whacky mind-set at the time, I was still affronted by this cavalier and irrelevant conversation taking place as I lay there, hurting and frightened. Their patter continued as though I didn't exist.

Linda could not understand the Indian doctors she had to deal with, and she asked Dr. Krumholtz to call them, to ascertain what exactly was happening. He called those doctors and reported back that he, too, was unable to understand what they said.

Needing an update, needing an outlook, a prognosis, Linda called the chief of neurology at Jackson who said he was too busy to see her, but could arrange a meeting at 8AM on Saturday morning. Linda arrived on time and entered the doctor's office. With malignant directness, he said, "Your husband is going to die!" and he walked out of the office.

I can only imagine the horror she felt, the sense of emptiness, shock, bewilderment, confusion and anger she experienced.

But Linda, being Linda, gathered her wits about her and, knowing the extremely poor care I'd received at Jackson, arranged to have me returned to Boca Regional hospital, where the nursing care was light-years better than in Miami.

Apparently, the insurance company, facing my ever increasing medical bills, decided that I would never recover and should be placed in a nursing facility where, I assume, I would be left to die on my own. Linda would not accept that and she manipulated my being transferred to the Pinecrest Rehabilitation Center in Delray Beach, one of the area's premier rehab facilities.

They turned me every few hours to avoid more bedsores, (as well as treated the bedsores sustained at Jackson) but everything had to be done for me, even brushing my teeth and shaving. While I couldn't speak, I could whisper and I could blink my eyes, so I devised a crude and primitive means of "conversing" with people. One blink for YES, two for NO. At least, I could communicate. And my daughter, Elizabeth, was the master at reading my lips.

Weeks later, I developed blood clots in my legs and was rushed to the emergency room in Delray Medical Center at midnight where they performed some procedure to alleviate the problem - I remember the young doctor complaining that it was late and he'd wanted to get home earlier. Of course, I couldn't even reply to apologize for his inconvenience, nor should I even have wished to. Sometimes silence can be golden, but only when you want it!

Shortly thereafter, I was awakened in the dead of night and taken to what seemed like a subterranean facility, where a powerful aide would pound my back for what seemed hours; this was repeated for about a week (I believe). I later learned that this was an attempt to avert the pneumonia which ultimately invaded my body. Something else to contend with. It seemed that as one problem was solved, another cropped up to take its place. It was discouraging, and it was frightening because there seemed to be no light at the end of the tunnel.

Rosh Hashana rolled around and an itinerant rabbi appeared in the doorway of my room, asking if I was Jewish. I couldn't answer. Ignoring my silence, he began liturgical chanting. I was never a ritualistic or practicing Jew, but somehow the cadence and melancholy of his prayers touched something deep in my soul and I interpreted his chanting as a dirge, a ceremony presaging my death.

The week before Thanksgiving, things took a turn for the worse. My body was so compromised that even with the feeding tube and the respirator, all efforts seemed insufficient to even to sustain me, much less promote any improvement.

My children and some close friends were called down to await my imminent death. I recall seeing them at my bedside, somber faced, anxious, and I sensed that my end was near.

But the crisis passed. At least, that crisis passed.

When the immune system is compromised, the body simply can't fight off ancillary infections and conditions; I now developed MRSA, a persistent and extremely serious staph infection, so infectious that nurses and visitors to my room were required to wear masks, and anything used to feed me was disposable plastic. In between meals, my mouth was swabbed with an antibiotic liquid. This lasted for weeks.

I knew that we were in the month of December, our anniversary and Linda's birthday. I needed to get cards for her. I was able to whisper to one wonderful young nurse what I needed and she arrived a few days later with two cards. She guided my hand as I scrawled, "Love, Steve" at the bottom of each card. I fell back on my pillows, so relieved that at least I was able to take care of that so important chore.

Throughout my ordeal, I focused on one thought: I would walk my daughter, Elizabeth, down the aisle at her wedding. Throughout various stages of my confinement, I altered the dream to my escorting her down the aisle in a wheelchair, although not my first choice.

But gradually, after December, after I'd given Linda her cards and Linda had brought each nurse a special coffee mug for Christmas, there were signs of improvement. I was taken off the nasal feed tube and the respirator, and begun on solid foods (actually, chocolate ice cream, after having been tested with snippets of food to see if my system would accept it or if I would choke). The paralysis was also beginning to retreat, moving down from my head gradually to the torso and arms. It is in the nature of Guillain-Barré to progress and retrogress thus - it begins at the feet and works its way up, and then, once recovery has begun, it reverses its direction for healing.

At about the same time, it was decided that I should graduate from lying on the special aero-mattress into a wheelchair but first they had to assess my body's acceptance of vertical positioning. I was placed on a long board which could gradually be raised to varying angles of elevation.

Strapped to the board, with a sphygmomanometer on my arm, the incline was slowly begun, and my blood pressure quickly began to plummet, so I was back down flat on my back. It took a week to get me to an elevation level where it was deemed safe to transfer me to a wheelchair, a painful step towards recovery. I had fallen to 138 pounds from 178 and my rear end was almost bony - sitting on it for the first time in months the pain was horrendous. You might ask how they knew my weight - simple. They wheeled me to a scale, lifted me on, subtracted the known poundage of the wheelchair and there you had it!

And my feet. In all those months, they'd never touched the floor; at night they were encased in wooden frames to prevent me from developing dropped foot, and now, for the first time, they were sporting sneakers and resting on the footpads of the wheelchair, and it was agony, like walking on coals, or a bed of knives. I whimpered, I pleaded to be put back on the comfortable bed, but it was not allowed.

Now that I was mobile, endless rounds of physical therapy began in earnest. Down in the "gym" I was placed on a low-lying cot, where the therapist began stretching me, the range of motion exercises which would bring back the elasticity of my muscles, if not yet the strength. This had been administered during my bedridden phase, but the regimen was now intensified.

Gradually, ever so gradually, my range of motion increased and I was started on a program of muscle strengthening - mainly weights for the arms and torso. Every morning I was taken down to the gym for the required stretching and exercising, and I was also beginning to stay alert enough to actually know and control what I was doing.

Throughout the many months, aside from bathing me, the nurses had been shaving me and brushing my teeth. But I could feel how desperately I need a haircut. The woman who regularly cut my hair agreed to come to the hospital and I was wheeled over to a sink in my room, with a mirror. It was the first time I'd seen myself since taking ill, and I was shocked at how gaunt, ashen and sick I really looked - also, how really badly I needed that haircut. She was wonderful and when she left, after sweeping up enough hair to make a crib mattress, I felt clean and, after those many months, almost normal.

At this time, the nurses alerted Linda to some strange stroking motions I was making. "Of course, " Linda explained, "He's stroking our cat." Agatha, our Siamese, was one of the loves of my life and while the stroking was unconscious, I certainly missed her. It was arranged to have me taken outside in my wheelchair, with portable oxygen apparatus, and have Agatha visit.

At the first try, I got violently dizzy in the wheelchair and suffered an anxiety attack, requiring me to be put back to bed immediately. The second time, I managed to stay in control and I was wheeled outside to be with my little "kitten" (actually several years old). Glorious, affectionate Agatha, that feisty, active, romping, miracle pet sat on my lap for an hour, purring as though willing me to get better by her very close presence as I stroked her and brushed away the loose hair that I hadn't brushed for months.

Normally she might have leaped from my lap and run through the grass chasing imaginary prey, but she didn't move that day.

This was the first bright spot, the first highlight of my hospitalization up until then. It was exhausting, but what a lift it gave me, what pure, quiet pleasure I derived from my little Agatha. She's gone, now, but I will always remember her and, especially, that rehab visit.

Once I was able to speak, I badgered the nurses and the therapists with one question: will I be able to walk? No one would, or could, give me a definitive answer, but my regimen clearly was geared to someone who might never walk again.

I was taken to the facility kitchen where I was taught how to maneuver cabinets, dishes and even cooking - I was assigned to make bacon and eggs, all from my chair. I tried to explain that I needn't bother because I had someone to cook for me, which fell on deaf ears.

I was taught how to manipulate myself from the wheelchair onto the bed with a wooden slide.

I was taken to Publix to conduct a "shopping tour," selecting products from various shelves and freezers to acclimate myself to handicapped life. I resented that phrase. I had been taken out one evening for dinner at a restaurant, in my wheelchair, ands became painfully aware of how patrons consciously averted their eyes from me, having taken in instantly that I was unable to walk. I felt, in their eyes, less than, something to be shunned, like the lepers in Medieval times, where people crossed the street to avoid the poor sufferers who were required to wear bells announcing their unwholesome and contagious condition.

Obviously, I would be able to manage myself from the confines of a wheelchair, not exactly what I wanted, but at least a viable option, given the potential limitation of my recovery.

I was also eating up a storm. Famished for real food and with an unlimited menu at my disposal, I was ordering two hamburgers for lunch and dinner, along with chocolate ice cream to settle my stomach (sic!) and my lost weight was rapidly coming back.

Still confined to the wheelchair, in February I was in the gym doing a prescribed exercise - leaning forward on a very large inflated ball and rolling forward. As I rolled back, my hands still on the ball, I stood! I actually stood. And at that moment, I knew I would walk again.

From that day on, therapy moved geometrically faster. I was graduated to periods of walking with crutches, I walked between parallel bars, and I was hoisted into and out of the pool, where (relatively weightless) I did walking exercises with the therapist beside me. My spirits improved, I was actually impatient to get down to the gym and strengthen my legs, strengthening my arms and torso by virtue of manipulating the wheelchair on my own.

My re-introduction to normalcy was accelerating. Now partly on crutches and alternately in the wheelchair, I was taken to our home where I was shown how to conduct leg exercises from the steps in our pool. Special seats were installed in our bathroom for maneuvering the toilet and the walk-in-shower.

I dreamed of leaving Pinecrest walking on my own, and I knew now this was an attainable goal. I also now knew that I would be able to walk my daughter down the aisle at her wedding. In April, I was discharged from the rehab hospital. With new braces on my legs and standing on my crutches, I waited impatiently for Linda to swing around with the car. The moment was at hand - I walked out of Pinecrest and back to my former life after nine months of hospitalization, fully cognizant that total normalcy was now something that would inevitably be mine, it was just a matter of time.

In the subsequent weeks, a physical therapist came to our home to provide exercises and evaluate my progress. Given all I'd been through, I was doing exceptionally well, but regaining full use of my legs without any aids was a slow process.

Shortly after I left Pinecrest in April of 1993, the family was invited to my father-in-law's presentation of Mt. Sinai Hospitals' Jacobi medallion in New York. Of course, I had to travel with and use my wheelchair.

Up until the night of the dinner at the Plaza, it was all pretty smooth sailing. I was dressed in my old tuxedo which hung on me like a Charlie Chaplin costume, and the family group photo taken before we left for the hotel shows me, even with some significant weight gain, to be a pale, cadaverous middle-aged man in a too big suit with a too-large shirt and a death-head smile. My body had simply not yet adapted itself back to its previous condition.

The limousine arrived and we drove to 59th street and Fifth Avenue and that's where the problem began. There was no way we could manage the wheelchair up the several steps into the Plaza lobby, but the hotel staff advised that we could enter on 58th street where there were no stairs. We drove around the block, found the proper door and entered. We were in the middle of the hotel kitchen. Since there was no elevator there leading to the Grand Ballroom, four waiters were assigned to CARRY me up the service stairs to the Grand Ballroom, after which, we all enjoyed the festivities and the honor of the occasion.

Heading home, the waiters carried me down and into the waiting car.

As my therapy progressed, I was also tested to see if I could drive a car. I was suffering (and still do) residual neuropathy in my feet. I still can't stand with my eyes closed or I will topple over. If I need to scan the evening sky for stars, or shampoo my hair, I need to lean on someone or something, a small price to pay for what might have resulted in permanent paralysis or even death.

I failed the first test because I couldn't switch my right leg from the gas pedal to the brake quickly enough. It took practice to regain that critical skill in order to operate a car.

In October, I was well enough and confident enough to start thinking about securing a job. Driving along Federal Highway, I noticed a building with the name, LABOR WORLD at its portal. I parked and, still walking with difficulty, I mounted the steps and went to the reception desk, where I asked the name of the president. Name in hand, I returned home, wrote a letter and, within two weeks, was interviewed and hired as the Senior Vice President for Strategic Communications at Labor World, a position I held and enjoyed for almost three years.

I was, at last, back to normal.

What do I most remember about my ordeal, and this I remember accurately and clearly?

Linda, my guardian angel, my advocate, bringing fresh flowers to me every Friday, visiting me every single day, encouraging me every day, interceding with professionals who were not doing their jobs properly to help me, and seeing to it that my care was paramount in her life as well as mine, fighting insurance people who simply wanted me dumped into a nursing home to die, fending off her own father from his false accusation about me, arranging for that seminal haircut, cosseting the entire nursing staff so they would give me special attention, bringing Agatha to comfort me, and being there for me to see, even when I couldn't move or speak, holding my inert hand, and kissing my forehead because my mouth was engaged with the respirator tube. For all of this, and so much more, I literally owe her my life!

My daughter, Elizabeth, working in New York, came almost every other weekend to visit me and support Linda. She also developed those charts with her mother that helped me identify, without benefit of speech, what basic needs I was addressing.

And the incredible magnanimity of my son, David, who came to Florida as often as his first year law school schedule would allow. He also volunteered to spend his summer vacation in Florida with us to help me and his mother maneuver around a still in recovery household. David lifted me, drove me, put up with my complaints and selfish demands. I'm certain he also defused more than a few tense moments with Linda who, while a paragon of selfless devotion, could get pretty fed up with me and my idiosyncrasies, some illness-induced, some merely genetic. Given David's generosity in burying himself in the Florida heat for two months, we learned quickly to overlook the early morning departures of ghostly female forms, and even the sight of some later exits, which warranted mutually embarrassing "good mornings."

Along with friends and some extraordinary medical practitioners, my family brought me back from the brink of death. This was the true test of family coming together in a crisis with love, advocacy and tenacity. And that is why I am here to pen this memoir.

Postscript

I N JULY OF 1992 I was between jobs and saw a small ad in the newspaper that caught my eye - A B'nai Brith health insurance policy at an affordable price. I signed up for the policy at the end of July.

As noted, my Guillain Barré experience lasted from September 1992 to April 1993. The total health costs amounted to $770,000, of which we were liable for $12,000.

Months later, that insurance company went bankrupt.

About The Author

S TEVE KATES, A NATIVE NEW Yorker residing in Florida for the past 26 years, came to writing after a lengthy career in the advertising agency business in New York City, and various positions in South Florida, retiring in 2000 as Chief Operating Officer of Fit America, Inc. in Deerfield Beach.

He then returned to his first love, writing, and was a film critic and features writer for ten years at the Boca Raton OBSERVER. Kates heads a small company devoted to editing, ghost writing and private writing seminars. He is also a Board member of the Institute for Learning in Retirement in Boca Raton, where he teaches, pro bono, seminars in Memoir and Short Story writing.

His first book of short works, LENGTH DOESN'T MATTER was published in 2014, followed by IN OTHER WORDS in 2015.

He and his wife, Linda, an Interior Designer, reside in Boca Raton, as does their daughter, Elizabeth and her husband and two daughters. Their son, David, lives in Sands Point, New York with his wife and two sons. Steve and Linda enjoy extensive world travel, family and tennis.

Printed in the United States
By Bookmasters